YOU ARE
COVERED

A JOURNEY OF PRAYER

MARIA CALHOUN

WestBow
PRESS®
A DIVISION OF THOMAS NELSON
& ZONDERVAN

WestBow Press books may be ordered through booksellers or by contacting:

WestBow Press
A Division of Thomas Nelson & Zondervan
1663 Liberty Drive
Bloomington, IN 47403
www.westbowpress.com
844-714-3454

Cover Design: Madison J Henry

ISBN: 978-1-6642-1935-9 (sc)
ISBN: 978-1-6642-1934-2 (e)

Print information available on the last page.

WestBow Press rev. date: 01/25/2021

It is okay to pray for you. It is a privilege to pray for others but we also need to cover ourselves. We need to be intentional about praying for ourselves.

This workbook is designed to take you on a journey that leads you to the feet of Jesus for you. There, you will place your heart concerns for yourself. At the back, I have included several journal pages for you to continue to write out prayers for yourself at the end of our journey together. Behind each week's journey you will find a blank journal page to write prayers to God about and for you. But before we do that, we need to take a moment, review our schedule and pinpoint a consistent time to pray for you.

Let's begin our journey. Grab your calendar and let's see what time you have available.

List your schedule

4:00

5:00

6:00

7:00

8:00

9:00

10:00

11:00

12:00 PM

1:00

2:00

3:00

4:00

5:00

6:00

7:00

8:00

9:00

10:00

11:00

12:00

Let's pause now and pray. Let's pray for God to reveal a time in your schedule for you to come before His throne of grace and boldly pray for yourself. God, through the Holy Spirit may reveal the time immediately or it may take some time. Review the schedule and highlight 3 time slots where you can pray for you.

WEEK 1

DAY ONE

Read Genesis 24.

Abraham requested that his servant find a wife for his son, Isaac, from among his own people. He asked him to swear that he would not find a Canaanite wife for his son but instead would find one of Abraham's relatives. This is a tremendous task. Can you imagine, being asked by your manager to find a wife for his son? I'm sure this was a stressful moment.

1. What was the servant's response to Abraham? (verse 5)

2. What concerns would you have had regarding this request?

3. Who did Abraham say would help his servant with this task? (verse7)

4. What does the servant do? (verse 12)

5. What task have you been asked to complete? Perhaps, you've been given a huge assignment at work. Maybe you have a newborn and you're getting less sleep now. You may have taken on a new ministry responsibility. Whatever it is, think of a task you're facing and let's pray for God to grant you success. Write out your prayer. Be specific.

DAY TWO

Read Genesis 24: 10-16

1. Write out Genesis 24: 15a:

2. Describe a time when God has answered your prayer immediately.

3. What stands out to you about the servant's prayer?

4. How does the servant's prayer encourage you?

Spend a few minutes meditating on Genesis 24:15-16.

Pray for God to give you a heart that is sensitive to His response to your prayers.

DAY THREE

Read: Genesis 24: 17-27

Write out verse 26.

1. How often do you stop to praise God for answered prayer?

2. List below three prayers that God has answered for you:

3. Write a prayer of praise for the prayers answered above.

4. What are your key takeaways from today's Scripture Text (Genesis 24: 17-27)?

Pray for God to enable you to remember to praise Him after answered prayers.

DAY FOUR

Read Genesis 24: 28-66

1. How would you describe the servant's performance for the task Abraham gave him?

2. List 3 key takeaways from today's Scripture reading:

1.

2.

3.

3. Based on the servant's testimony (verses 34-48), what did this confirm to Laban and Bethuel (verse 50)?

As God begins to answer the prayers you pray for yourself, this will become a testimony. Be prepared to share your testimony with others.

Pray for God to give you a bold spirit to share your testimony with others.

DAY FIVE

1. Select a portion of Scripture from Genesis 24 to meditate on.

2. How has God spoken to you during your time in prayer this week?

3. How has the Scripture we covered today transformed your view of praying for yourself?

Find time today and over the weekend to pray over any issue that is pressing on your heart regarding yourself.

Heavenly Father:

WEEK TWO

DAY ONE

Read 1 Samuel 1

Hannah's situation left her in tears. She was troubled by what may have felt like a losing situation. She was taunted by her rival (1 Samuel 1:7). Her rival was a constant reminder of her lack, her need and disappointment. Scripture tells us she was taunted for quite some time. Her situation had taken her appetite. She was sad and possibly overwhelmed with disappointment.

1. What was Hannah's need/lack?

2. Describe Hannah's situation.

3. How would you advise Hannah?

4. What did Hannah do about her situation? (verse 10)

5. How did Hannah describe her situation? (verse 15)

6. What situation has left you in great anguish or grief?

7. Whatever situation is currently causing you stress or anguish, let's pray for God to send deliverance and healing:

DAY TWO

Read 1 Samuel 1: 3-8

1. What was Elkanah's response to Hannah?

2. Was his response sufficient? Why or why not?

3. Can you think of time when the response of other's was not sufficient (in your opinion) for you? Why not?

4. What do you find most heartbreaking about Hannah's situation?

5. Write a prayer asking God to grant you discernment on how to respond to others in need.

DAY THREE

Read 1 Samuel 1: 9-18

1. How do verses 9-18 describe Hannah's emotional condition?

2. What did Hannah do in response to her emotional condition?

3. Describe a situation/hardship that drained you emotionally. Did you cover it in prayer?

4. Is there a situation that is currently pressing on your heart? Use this section to write out a prayer to our loving Heavenly Father.

5. Write out and meditate on Isaiah 65:24.

DAY FOUR

Read 1 Samuel 1:19-28

1. Describe what happens in verses 19-20.

2. How would you describe your worship life?

3. When going through a challenging time, do you find it difficult to worship? Why or why not?

4. Once Hannah, brought her child to Eli how did she remind him of who she was (verse 26)?

5. God granted Hannah's request. How did she keep her commitment to the Lord?

DAY FIVE

Hannah worshipped. Today, we will use this time to worship and pray. Find a worship song/hymn that speaks to your heart. As the song plays, pray for God to give you a heart of worship.

Write about your experience below:

Father of Peace and Strength:

WEEK THREE

DAY ONE

Read 2 Kings 20: 1-11

1. Read and write below 2 Kings 20:2-3.

2. What prompted Hezekiah to pray for himself?

3. Before Hezekiah prays, he turns away from what is around him to face the wall (2 Kings 20:2). Why do you think he turned his face to the wall? What impact do you think it had on his time with the Lord?

4. How can you prepare for a time of prayer?

5. What were the contents of Hezekiah's prayer?

6. Plan time today to turn your face to the wall and seek the Lord. Write about your experience below.

DAY TWO

1. Based on your time with the Lord yesterday (question 6 from Day 1), how did the content of your prayer compare to Hezekiah's?

2. Read 2 Kings 20: 4-6

What happened after Hezekiah prayed?

3. What have you seen happen after you have prayed?

4. What encouragement do you receive from God's response to Hezekiah's prayer?

5. Let's end our time together praying for God to give you a heart that is sensitive to His response to your prayer.

DAY THREE

Read 2 Kings 20: 7-11

1. Why do you believe Hezekiah asked for a sign?

2. After you submit your prayer requests to God, what do you typically do next? How does it compare to Hezekiah's actions after he prayed?

3. How did the Lord respond to Hezekiah's request for a sign?

4. Based on verses 7-11, what attributes of God do you see?

5. What attributes of God's character do you need to experience more of today? Let's cover it in prayer below.

DAY FOUR

Read 2 Kings 20:4-5

1. Write out 2 Kings 20:5.

2. God hears our prayers. Is there a situation you're currently covering in prayer for yourself and God appears silent?

3. Search scripture for obstacles to prayers and list them below.

4. Are any of the obstacles listed above true in your life? If so, let's confess those to God and cover in prayer.

DAY FIVE

1. Review 2 Kings 20:1-11. How has this Scripture text encouraged you to pray more for yourself?

2. Which area of your life have you covered the least in prayer? Why?

3. Let's use this section to cover in prayer that area in your life that needs it the most (see answer to question 2).

God of Mercy and Grace:

WEEK FOUR

We have come to our final week of You Are Covered. We are going to read a passage of Scripture that allows us to witness Jesus praying for Himself.

DAY ONE

Read Matthew 26: 36-46

1. Where did Jesus go? Who went with him?

2. Look up details in a commentary/concordance or Study Bible regarding Gethsemane and list below any details you discover about Gethsemane.

3. Describe the place where you go to pray.

4. What was Jesus' physical or emotional condition as He entered Gethsemane?

5. Describe the content of Jesus' prayer.

6. What stands out to you about Jesus' prayer.

DAY TWO

Read Matthew 26: 36-39

1. Write out verse 39.

2. Describe Jesus' physical position for prayer. Why do you think he assumed this position?

3. What physical positions do you have while praying? Is the physical position of prayer important to you? Why?

4. Jesus prays for the Father's will to be done. When you pray, do you surrender to the Father's will? Why or why not?

5. Let's end today in prayer. Pray for God to speak to your heart about His will for your life.

DAY THREE

Read Matthew 26:40-41

1. Write out Matthew 26:40-41.

2. What were the disciples doing in verse 40 and what was Jesus' response?

3. What steps have you taken to remain focused during prayer?

4. What did Jesus mean when He said "The spirit is willing, but the flesh is weak(Matthew 26:41c.)"?

5. What has been your experience when asking others to pray for you?

DAY FOUR

Read Matthew 26:42-46

1. Jesus said to His Father, "My Father, if it is not possible for this cup to be taken away unless I drink it, may your will be done(Matthew 26:42)." What situation are you struggling with right now?

2. Based on the situation you listed in question 1, write a prayer of surrender to God's will.

3. Have you ever asked someone to pray for you and with you but they failed to do so? Have you ever failed to pray for someone? What prevented you from praying for them?

4. Notice that even though Jesus had brought others with him to pray, He still prayed for Himself. Why was this important?

DAY FIVE

Congrats! You made it to the final day of our time together. Prayerfully, you are starting to pray more for yourself. We explored how Abraham's servant, Hannah, King Hezekiah and Jesus prayed for themselves. Today, you will spend time praying for you. Let's do it!

1. Find Scripture that speak to one of the following:

    a. Something you are struggling with
    b. A need you may have
    c. A spiritual area you are interested in growing in

2. Once you have the Scripture, use the space below to pray that Scripture over you.

3. Of the biblical characters discussed (Abraham's servant, Hannah, King Hezekiah and Jesus) which one were you most inspired by and why?

4. God has an assignment for all of His children. Use the space below to pray for God to open your eyes to the assignment He has for you.

5. What has interfered with your time in prayer for yourself? Use the space below to pray for God to give you uninterrupted time in prayer for yourself.

Lord:

ABOUT THE AUTHOR

Maria Calhoun enjoys spending time with her husband, Clyde, serving in the body of Christ and taking long walks. She has facilitated various bible studies. She has a B.A in Communications from Winthrop University and a Master of Business Administration from Lincoln Memorial University. Her passion is encouraging women to spend consistent time in prayer and God's Word. She hosts a weekly podcast, You Are Covered , which encourages her audience to be intentional about praying for themselves.

EXTRA JOURNALING PAGES

Printed in the United States
By Bookmasters